THE GOSPEL OF JOHN

The Word of Life

1 Before the world was created, the Word already existed; he was with God, and he was the same as God. [2] From the very beginning, the Word was with God. [3] Through him God made all things; not one thing in all creation was made without him. [4] The Word had life in himself, and this life brought light to men. [5] The light shines in the darkness, and the darkness has never put it out.

[6] God sent his messenger, a man named John, [7] who came to tell people about the light. He came to tell them, so that all should hear the message and believe. [8] He himself was not the light; he came to tell about the light. [9] This was the real light, the light that comes into the world and shines on all men.

[10] The Word, then, was in the world. God made the world through him, yet the world did not know him. [11] He came to his own country, but his own people did not receive him. [12] Some, however, did receive him and believed in him; so he gave them the right to become God's children. [13] They did not become God's children by natural means, by being born as the children of a human father; God himself was their Father.

[14] The Word became a human being and lived among us. We saw his glory, full of grace and truth. This was the glory which he received as the Father's only Son.

[15] John told about him. He cried out, "This is the one I was talking about when I said, 'He comes after me, but he is greater than I am, because he existed before I was born.'"

[16] Out of the fulness of his grace he has blessed us all, giving us one blessing after another. [17] God gave the Law through Moses; but grace and truth came through Jesus Christ. [18] No one has ever seen God. The only One, who is the same as God and is at the Father's side, he has made him known.

John the Baptist's Message
(Also Matt. 3.1–12; Mark 1.1–8; Luke 3.1–18)

[19] This is what John said when the Jews in Jerusalem sent priests and Levites to ask him, "Who are you?"

[20] John did not refuse to answer, but declared openly and clearly, "I am not the Messiah." [21] "Who are you, then?" they asked. "Are you Elijah?" "No, I am not," John answered. "Are you the Prophet?" they asked. "No," he replied. [22] "Tell us who you are," they said. "We have to take an answer back to those who sent us. What do you say about yourself?" [23] John answered, "This is what I am:

'The voice of one who shouts in the desert:
Make a straight path for the Lord to travel!' "
(This is what the prophet Isaiah had said.)

[24] The messengers had been sent by the Pharisees. [25] They asked John, "If you are not the Messiah, nor Elijah, nor the Prophet, why do you baptize?" [26] John answered: "I baptize with water; among you stands the one you do not know. [27] He comes after me, but I am not good enough even to untie his sandals."

[28] All this happened in Bethany, on the other side of the Jordan river, where John was baptizing.

The Lamb of God

[29] The next day John saw Jesus coming to him and said: "Here is the Lamb of God who takes away the sin of the world! [30] This is the one I was talking about when I said, 'A man comes after me, but he is greater than I am, because he existed before I was born.' [31] I did not know who he would be, but I came baptizing with water in order to make him known to Israel."

[32] This is the testimony that John gave: "I saw the Spirit come down like a dove from heaven and stay on him. [33] I still did not know him, but God, who sent me to baptize with water, said to me, 'You will see the Spirit come down and stay on a

GOOD NEWS
TOLD BY JOHN

Today's English Version

THE BRITISH AND
FOREIGN BIBLE SOCIETY
THE NATIONAL BIBLE
SOCIETY OF SCOTLAND

in association with
COLLINS
Fontana books

Price 3p.
*This price is made possible
by the subsidy of the Bible Societies*

English—John TEV—560P
BFBS/NBSS—1971—100M
ISBN 0 564 06501 3

© *American Bible Society, New York*
1966

Printed in Great Britain
Collins Clear-Type Press
London and Glasgow
in association with the
British and Foreign Bible Society
146 Queen Victoria Street, London, E.C.4
and the
National Bible Society of Scotland
5 St. Andrew Square, Edinburgh, 2

man; he is the one who baptizes with the Holy Spirit.' ³⁴ I have seen it," said John, "and I tell you that he is the Son of God."

The First Disciples of Jesus

³⁵ The next day John was there again with two of his disciples, ³⁶ when he saw Jesus walking by. "Here is the Lamb of God!" he said. ³⁷ The two disciples heard him say this and went with Jesus. ³⁸ Jesus turned, saw them following him, and asked, "What are you looking for?" They answered, "Where do you live, Rabbi?" (This word, translated, means "Teacher.") ³⁹ "Come and see," he answered. So they went with him and saw where he lived, and spent the rest of that day with him. (It was about four o'clock in the afternoon.)

⁴⁰ One of the two who heard John, and went with Jesus, was Andrew, Simon Peter's brother. ⁴¹ At once Andrew found his brother Simon and told him, "We have found the Messiah." (This word means "Christ.") ⁴² Then he brought Simon to Jesus. Jesus looked at him and said, "You are Simon, the son of John. Your name will be Cephas." (This is the same as Peter, and means "Rock.")

Jesus Calls Philip and Nathanael

⁴³ The next day Jesus decided to go to Galilee. He found Philip and said to him, "Come with me!" ⁴⁴ (Philip was from Bethsaida, the town where Andrew and Peter lived.) ⁴⁵ So Philip found Nathanael and told him: "We have found the one of whom Moses wrote in the book of the Law, and of whom the prophets also wrote. He is Jesus, the son of Joseph, from Nazareth." ⁴⁶ "Can anything good come from Nazareth?" Nathanael asked. "Come and see," answered Philip.

⁴⁷ When Jesus saw Nathanael coming to him, he said about him, "Here is a real Israelite; there is nothing false in him!" ⁴⁸ Nathanael asked him, "How do you know me?" Jesus answered, "I saw you when you were under the fig tree, before Philip called you." ⁴⁹ "Teacher," answered Nathanael, "you are the Son of God! You are the King of Israel!" ⁵⁰ Jesus said, "Do you believe just because I told you I saw you when you were under the fig tree? You will see much greater things than this!" ⁵¹ And

he said to them, "I tell you the truth: you will see heaven open and God's angels going up and coming down on the Son of Man!"

The Wedding at Cana

2 Two days later there was a wedding in the town of Cana, in Galilee. Jesus' mother was there, ² and Jesus and his disciples had also been invited to the wedding. ³ When all the wine had been drunk, Jesus' mother said to him, "They are out of wine." ⁴ "You must not tell me what to do, woman," Jesus replied. "My time has not yet come." ⁵ Jesus' mother then told the servants, "Do whatever he tells you."

⁶ The Jews have religious rules about washing, and for this purpose six stone water jars were there, each one large enough to hold between twenty and thirty gallons. ⁷ Jesus said to the servants, "Fill these jars with water." They filled them to the brim, ⁸ and then he told them, "Now draw some water out and take it to the man in charge of the feast." They took it to him, ⁹ and he tasted the water, which had turned into wine. He did not know

where this wine had come from (but the servants who had drawn out the water knew); so he called the bridegroom 10 and said to him, "Everyone else serves the best wine first, and after the guests have drunk a lot he serves the ordinary wine. But you have kept the best wine until now!"

11 Jesus performed this first of his mighty works in Cana of Galilee; there he revealed his glory, and his disciples believed in him.

12 After this, Jesus and his mother, brothers, and disciples went to Capernaum, and stayed there a few days.

Jesus Goes to the Temple
(Also Matt. 21.12–13; Mark 11.15–17; Luke 19.45–46)

13 It was almost time for the Jewish Feast of Passover, so Jesus went to Jerusalem. 14 In the Temple he found men selling cattle, sheep, and pigeons, and also the money-changers sitting at their tables. 15 He made a whip from cords and drove all the animals out of the Temple, both the sheep and the cattle; he overturned the tables of the money-changers and scattered their coins; 16 and he ordered the men who sold the pigeons, "Take them out of here! Do not make my Father's house a market place!" 17 His disciples remembered that the scripture says, "My devotion for your house, O God, burns in me like a fire."

18 The Jews came back at him with a question, "What miracle can you perform to show us that you have the right to do this?" 19 Jesus answered, "Tear down this house of God and in three days I will build it again." 20 "You

are going to build it again in three days?" they asked him. "It has taken forty-six years to build this Temple!" 21 But the temple Jesus spoke of was his body. 22 When he was raised from death, therefore, his disciples remembered that he said this; and they believed the scripture and the words that Jesus had said.

Jesus Knows All Men

23 While Jesus was in Jerusalem during the Passover Feast, many believed in him as they saw the mighty works he did. 24 But Jesus did not trust himself to them, because he knew all men well. 25 There was no need for anyone to tell him about men, for he well knew what goes on in their hearts.

Jesus and Nicodemus

3 There was a man named Nicodemus, a leader of the Jews, who belonged to the party of the Pharisees. 2 One night he came to Jesus and said to him: "We know, Rabbi, that you are a teacher sent by God. No one could do the mighty works you are doing unless God were with him." 3 Jesus answered, "I tell you the truth: no one can see the Kingdom of God unless he is born again." 4 "How can a grown man be born again?" Nicodemus asked. "He certainly cannot enter his mother's womb and be born a second time!" 5 "I tell you the truth," replied Jesus, "that no one can enter the Kingdom of God unless he is born of water and the Spirit. 6 Flesh gives birth to flesh, and Spirit gives birth to spirit. 7 Do not be surprised because I tell you, 'You must all be born again.' 8 The wind blows wherever it wishes; you hear the sound it makes, but you do not know where it comes from or where it is going. It is the same way with everyone who is born of the Spirit." 9 "How can this be?" asked Nicodemus. 10 Jesus answered: "You are a great teacher of Israel, and you don't know this? 11 I tell you the truth: we speak of what we know, and tell what we have seen — yet none of you is willing to accept our message. 12 You do not believe me when I tell you about the things of this world; how will you ever believe me, then, when I tell you about the things of heaven? 13 And no one has ever gone up to heaven except the Son of Man, who came down from heaven."

14 As Moses lifted up the bronze snake on a pole in the

desert, in the same way the Son of Man must be lifted up, [15] so that everyone who believes in him may have eternal life. [16] For God loved the world so much that he gave his only Son, so that everyone who believes in him may not die but have eternal life. [17] For God did not send his Son into the world to be its Judge, but to be its Saviour.

[18] Whoever believes in the Son is not judged; whoever does not believe has already been judged, because he has not believed in God's only Son. [19] This is how the judgment works: the light has come into the world, but men love the darkness rather than the light, because they do evil things. [20] And anyone who does evil things hates the light and will not come to the light, because he does not want his evil deeds to be shown up. [21] But whoever does what is true comes to the light, in order that the light may show that he did his works in obedience to God.

Jesus and John

[22] After this, Jesus and his disciples went to the province of Judea. He spent some time with them there, and baptized. [23] John also was baptizing in Aenon, not far from Salim, because there was plenty of water there. People were going to him and he was baptizing them. [24] (John had not yet been put in prison.)

[25] Some of John's disciples began arguing with a Jew about the matter of religious washing. [26] So they went to John and told him: "Teacher, you remember the man who was with you on the other side of the Jordan, the one you spoke about? Well, he is baptizing now, and everyone is going to him!" [27] John answered: "No one can have anything unless God gives it to him. [28] You yourselves are my witnesses that I said, 'I am not the Messiah, but I have been sent ahead of him.' [29] The bridegroom is the one to whom the bride belongs; the bridegroom's friend stands by and listens, and he is glad when he hears the bridegroom's voice. This is how my own happiness is made complete. [30] He must become more important, while I become less important."

He who Comes from Heaven

[31] He who comes from above is greater than all; he who is from the earth belongs to the earth and speaks about earthly matters. He who comes from heaven is above all.

[32] He tells what he has seen and heard, but no one accepts his message. [33] Whoever accepts his message proves by this that God is true. [34] The one whom God has sent speaks God's words; for God gives him the fulness of his Spirit. [35] The Father loves his Son and has put everything in his power. [36] Whoever believes in the Son has eternal life; whoever disobeys the Son will never have life, but God's wrath will remain on him for ever.

Jesus and the Woman of Samaria

4 The Pharisees heard that Jesus was winning and baptizing more disciples than John. [2] (Actually, Jesus himself did not baptize anyone; only his disciples did.) [3] When Jesus heard what was being said, he left Judea and went back to Galilee; [4] on his way there he had to go through Samaria.

[5] He came to a town in Samaria named Sychar, which was not far from the field that Jacob had given to his son Joseph. [6] Jacob's well was there, and Jesus, tired out by the journey, sat down by the well. It was about noon.

[7] A Samaritan woman came to draw some water, and Jesus said to her, "Give me a drink of water." [8] (His disciples had gone into town to buy food.) [9] The Samaritan woman answered, "You are a Jew and I am a Samaritan — how can you ask me for a drink?" (For Jews will not use the same dishes that Samaritans use.) [10] Jesus answered, "If you only knew what God gives, and who it is that is asking you for a drink, you would have asked

him and he would have given you living water." [11] "Sir," the woman said, "you don't have a bucket and the well is deep. Where would you get living water? [12] Our ancestor Jacob gave us this well; he, his sons, and his flocks all drank from it. You don't claim to be greater than Jacob, do you?" [13] Jesus answered: "Whoever drinks this water will get thirsty again; [14] but whoever drinks the water that I will give him will never be thirsty again. For the water that I will give him will become in him a spring which will provide him with living water, and give him eternal life." [15] "Sir," the woman said, "give me this water! Then I will never be thirsty again, nor will I have to come here and draw water." [16] "Go call your husband," Jesus told her, "and come back here." [17] "I haven't got a husband," the woman said. Jesus replied: "You are right when you say you haven't got a husband. [18] You have been married to five men, and the man you live with now is not really your husband. You have told me the truth." [19] "I see you are a prophet, sir," the woman said. [20] "My Samaritan ancestors worshipped God on this mountain, but you Jews say that Jerusalem is the place where we should worship God." [21] Jesus said to her: "Believe me, woman, the time will come when men will not worship the Father either on this mountain or in Jerusalem. [22] You Samaritans do not really know whom you worship; we Jews know whom we worship, for salvation comes from the Jews. [23] But the time is coming, and is already here, when the real worshippers will worship the Father in spirit and in truth. These are the worshippers the Father wants to worship him. [24] God is Spirit, and those who worship him must worship in spirit and in truth."

[25] The woman said to him, "I know that the Messiah, called Christ, will come. When he comes he will tell us everything." [26] Jesus answered, "I am he, I who am talking with you."

[27] At that moment Jesus' disciples returned; and they were greatly surprised to find him talking with a woman. But none of them said to her, "What do you want?" or asked him, "Why are you talking with her?"

[28] Then the woman left her water jar, went back to town, and said to the people there, [29] "Come and see the man who told me everything I have ever done. Could he be the Messiah?" [30] So they left the town and went to Jesus.

³¹ In the meantime the disciples were begging Jesus, "Teacher, have something to eat!" ³² But he answered, "I have food to eat that you know nothing about." ³³ So the disciples started asking among themselves, "Could somebody have brought him food?" ³⁴ "My food," Jesus said to them, "is to obey the will of him who sent me and finish the work he gave me to do.

³⁵ "You have a saying, 'Four more months and then the harvest.' I tell you, take a good look at the fields: the crops are now ripe and ready to be harvested! ³⁶ The man who reaps the harvest is being paid and gathers the crops for eternal life; so that the man who plants and the man who reaps will be glad together. ³⁷ For the saying is true, 'One man plants, another man reaps.' ³⁸ I have sent you to reap a harvest in a field where you did not work; others worked there, and you profit from their work."

³⁹ Many of the Samaritans in that town believed in Jesus because the woman had said, "He told me everything I have ever done." ⁴⁰ So when the Samaritans came to him they begged him to stay with them; and Jesus stayed there two days.

⁴¹ Many more believed because of his message, ⁴² and they told the woman, "We believe now, not because of what you said, but because we ourselves have heard him, and we know that he is really the Saviour of the world."

Jesus Heals an Official's Son

⁴³ After spending two days there, Jesus left and went to Galilee. ⁴⁴ For Jesus himself had said, "A prophet is not respected in his own country." ⁴⁵ When he arrived in Galilee the people there welcomed him, for they themselves had gone to the Passover Feast in Jerusalem and had seen everything that he had done during the feast.

⁴⁶ So Jesus went back to Cana of Galilee, where he had turned the water into wine. There was a government official there whose son in Capernaum was sick. ⁴⁷ When he heard that Jesus had come from Judea to Galilee, he went to him and asked him to go to Capernaum and heal his son, who was about to die. ⁴⁸ Jesus said to him, "None of you will ever believe unless you see great and wonderful works." ⁴⁹ "Sir," replied the official, "come with me before my child dies." ⁵⁰ Jesus said to him, "Go, your son will live!" The man believed Jesus' words and went. ⁵¹ On his

way home his servants met him with the news, "Your boy is going to live!" [52] He asked them what time it was when his son got better, and they said, "It was one o'clock yesterday afternoon when the fever left him." [53] The father remembered, then, that it was at that very hour when Jesus had told him, "Your son will live." So he and all his family believed.

[54] This was the second mighty work that Jesus did after coming from Judea to Galilee.

The Healing at the Pool

5 After this, there was a Jewish religious feast, and Jesus went to Jerusalem. [2] There is in Jerusalem, by the Sheep Gate, a pool with five porches; in the Hebrew language it is called Bethzatha. [3] A large crowd of sick people were lying on the porches — the blind, the lame, and the paralyzed. [They were waiting for the water to move; [4] for every now and then an angel of the Lord went down into the pool and stirred up the water. The first sick person to go down into the pool after the water was stirred up was healed from whatever disease he had.] [5] A man was there who had been sick for thirty-eight years. [6] Jesus saw him lying there, and he knew that the man had been sick for such a long time; so he said to him, "Do you want to get well?" [7] The sick man answered, "Sir, I don't have anyone here to put me in the pool when the water is stirred up; while I am trying to get in, somebody else gets there first." [8] Jesus said to him, "Get up, pick up your mat, and walk." [9] Immediately the man got well; he picked up his mat, and walked.

The day this happened was a Sabbath, [10] so the Jews told the man who had been healed, "This is a Sabbath, and it is against our Law for you to carry your mat." [11] He answered, "The man who made me well told me, 'Pick up your mat and walk.'" [12] They asked him, "Who is this man who told you to pick up your mat and walk?" [13] But the man who had been healed did not know who he was, for Jesus had left, because there was a crowd in that place.

[14] Afterward, Jesus found him in the Temple and said, "Look, you are well now. Quit your sins, or something worse may happen to you." [15] Then the man left and told the Jews that it was Jesus who had healed him. [16] For this

reason the Jews began to persecute Jesus, because he had done this healing on a Sabbath. [17] So Jesus answered them, "My Father works always, and I too must work." [18] This saying made the Jews all the more determined to kill him; for not only had he broken the Sabbath law, but he had said that God was his own Father, and in this way had made himself equal with God.

The Authority of the Son

[19] So Jesus answered them: "I tell you the truth: the Son does nothing on his own; he does only what he sees his Father doing. What the Father does, the Son also does. [20] For the Father loves the Son and shows him all that he himself is doing. He will show him even greater things than this to do, and you will all be amazed. [21] For even as the Father raises the dead back to life, in the same way the Son gives life to those he wants to. [22] Nor does the Father himself judge anyone. He has given his Son the full right to judge, [23] so that all will honour the Son in the same way as they honour the Father. Whoever does not honour the Son does not honour the Father who sent him.

[24] "I tell you the truth: whoever hears my words, and believes in him who sent me, has eternal life. He will not be judged, but has already passed from death to life. [25] I tell you the truth: the time is coming — the time has already come — when the dead will hear the voice of the Son of God, and those who hear it will live. [26] Even as the Father is himself the source of life, in the same way he has made his Son to be the source of life. [27] And he has given the Son the right to judge, because he is the Son of Man. [28] Do not be surprised at this; for the time is coming when all the dead in the graves will hear his voice, [29] and they will come out of their graves: those who have done good will be raised and live, and those who have done evil will be raised and be condemned."

Witnesses to Jesus

[30] "I can do nothing on my own; I judge only as God tells me, so my judgment is right, because I am not trying to do what I want, but only what he who sent me wants.

[31] "If I testify on my own behalf, what I say is not to be accepted as real proof. [32] But there is someone else who

testifies on my behalf, and I know that what he says about me is true. [33] You sent your messengers to John, and he spoke on behalf of the truth. [34] It is not that I must have a man's witness; I say this only in order that you may be saved. [35] John was like a lamp, burning and shining, and you were willing for a while to enjoy his light. [36] But I have a witness on my behalf even greater than the witness that John gave: the works that I do, the works my Father gave me to do, these speak on my behalf and show that the Father has sent me. [37] And the Father, who sent me, also speaks on my behalf. You have never heard his voice, you have never seen his face; [38] so you do not have his words in you, because you will not believe in the one whom he sent. [39] You study the Scriptures because you think that in them you will find eternal life. And they themselves speak about me! [40] Yet you are not willing to come to me in order to have life.

[41] "I am not looking for praise from men. [42] But I know you; I know that you have no love for God in your hearts. [43] I have come with my Father's authority, but you have not received me; when someone comes with his own authority, you will receive him. [44] You like to have praise from one another, but you do not try to win praise from the only God; how, then, can you believe? [45] Do not think, however, that I will accuse you to my Father. Moses is the one who will accuse you — Moses, in whom you have hoped. [46] If you had really believed Moses, you would have believed me, for he wrote about me. [47] But since you do not believe what he wrote, how can you believe my words?"

Jesus Feeds the Five Thousand
(Also Matt. 14.13–21; Mark 6.30–44; Luke 9.10–17)

6 After this, Jesus went back across Lake Galilee (or, Lake Tiberias). [2] A great crowd followed him, because they had seen his mighty works in healing the sick. [3] Jesus went up a hill and sat down with his disciples. [4] The Passover Feast of the Jews was near. [5] Jesus looked round and saw that a large crowd was coming to him, so he said to Philip, "Where can we buy enough food to feed all these people?" [6] (He said this to try Philip out; actually he already knew what he would do.) [7] Philip answered, "For all these people to have even a little, it would take

more than twenty pounds' worth of bread." ⁸ Another one of his disciples, Andrew, Simon Peter's brother, said: ⁹ "There is a boy here who has five loaves of barley bread and two fish. But what good are they for all these people?" ¹⁰ "Make the people sit down," Jesus told them. (There was a lot of grass around there.) So all the people sat down; there were about five thousand men. ¹¹ Jesus took the bread, gave thanks to God, and distributed it to the people sitting down. He did the same with the fish, and they all had as much as they wanted. ¹² When they were all full, he said to his disciples, "Pick up the pieces left over; let us not waste a bit." ¹³ So they took them all up, and filled twelves baskets full of pieces of the five barley loaves left over by those who ate.

¹⁴ The people there, seeing this mighty work that Jesus had done, said, "Surely this is the Prophet who was to come to the world!" ¹⁵ Jesus knew that they were about to come and get him and make him king by force; so he went off again to the hills by himself.

Jesus Walks on the Water
(Also Matt. 14.22–33; Mark 6.45–52)

¹⁶ When evening came, his disciples went down to the lake, ¹⁷ got into the boat, and went back across the lake toward Capernaum. Night came on, and Jesus still had not come to them. ¹⁸ By now a strong wind was blowing and stirring up the water. ¹⁹ The disciples had rowed

about three or four miles when they saw Jesus walking on the water, coming near the boat, and they were terrified. 20 "Don't be afraid," Jesus told them, "it is I!" 21 They were willing to take him into the boat; and immediately the boat reached land at the place they were heading for.

The People Seek Jesus

22 Next day the crowd which had stayed on the other side of the lake saw that only one boat was left there. They knew that Jesus had not gone in the boat with his disciples, but that they had left without him. 23 Other boats, from Tiberias, came to shore near the place where the crowd had eaten the bread, after the Lord had given thanks. 24 When the crowd saw that Jesus was not there, nor his disciples, they got into boats and went to Capernaum, looking for him.

Jesus the Bread of Life

25 When the people found Jesus on the other side of the lake they said to him, "Teacher, when did you get here?" 26 Jesus answered: "I tell you the truth: you are looking for me because you ate the bread and had all you wanted, not because you saw my works of power. 27 Do not work for food that spoils; instead, work for the food that lasts for eternal life. This food the Son of Man will give you, because God, the Father, has put his mark of approval on him." 28 They asked him then, "What can we do in order to do God's works?" 29 Jesus answered, "This is the work God wants you to do: believe in the one he sent." 30 They replied: "What sign of power will you perform so that we may see it and believe you? What will you do? 31 Our ancestors ate manna in the desert, just as the scripture says: 'He gave them bread from heaven to eat.'" 32 "I tell you the truth," Jesus said. "What Moses gave you was not the bread from heaven; it is my Father who gives you the real bread from heaven. 33 For the bread that God gives is he who comes down from heaven and gives life to the world." 34 "Sir," they asked him, "give us this bread always." 35 "I am the bread of life," Jesus told them. "He who comes to me will never be hungry; he who believes in me will never be thirsty.

36 "Now, I told you that you had seen me but would not believe. 37 Every one whom my Father gives me will come

to me. I will never turn away anyone who comes to me,
[38] for I have come down from heaven to do the will of him
who sent me, not my own will. [39] This is what he who sent
me wants me to do: that I should not lose any of all those
he has given me, but that I should raise them all to life on
the last day. [40] For this is what my Father wants: that all
who see the Son and believe in him should have eternal
life; and I will raise them to life on the last day."

[41] The Jews started grumbling about him, because he
said, "I am the bread that came down from heaven."
[42] So they said: "This man is Jesus the son of Joseph, isn't
he? We know his father and mother. How, then, does he
now say he came down from heaven?" [43] Jesus answered:
"Stop grumbling among yourselves. [44] No one can come
to me unless the Father who sent me draws him to me;
and I will raise him to life on the last day. [45] The prophets
wrote, 'All men will be taught by God.' Everyone who
hears the Father and learns from him comes to me.
[46] This does not mean that anyone has seen the Father; he
who is from God is the only one who has seen the Father.

[47] "I tell you the truth: he who believes has eternal life.
[48] I am the bread of life. [49] Your ancestors ate the manna
in the desert, but died. [50] But the bread which comes down
from heaven is such that whoever eats it will not die. [51] I
am the living bread which came down from heaven. If
anyone eats this bread he will live for ever. And the bread
which I will give him is my flesh, which I give so that the
world may live."

[52] This started an angry argument among the Jews.
"How can this man give us his flesh to eat?" they asked.
[53] Jesus said to them: "I tell you the truth: if you do not
eat the flesh of the Son of Man and drink his blood you
will not have life in yourselves. [54] Whoever eats my flesh
and drinks my blood has eternal life, and I will raise him
to life on the last day. [55] For my flesh is the real food, my
blood is the real drink. [56] Whoever eats my flesh and
drinks my blood lives in me and I live in him. [57] The living Father sent me, and because of him I live also. In the
same way, whoever eats me will live because of me.
[58] This, then, is the bread that came down from heaven; it
is not like the bread that your ancestors ate and then died.
The one who eats this bread will live for ever." [59] Jesus
said this as he taught in the synagogue in Capernaum.

The Words of Eternal Life

⁶⁰ Many of his disciples heard this and said, "This teaching is too hard. Who can listen to this?" ⁶¹ Without being told, Jesus knew that his disciples were grumbling about this; so he said to them: "Does this make you want to give up? ⁶² Suppose, then, that you should see the Son of Man go back up to the place where he was before? ⁶³ What gives life is the Spirit; the flesh is of no use at all. The words I have spoken to you are Spirit and life. ⁶⁴ Yet some of you do not believe." (For Jesus knew from the very beginning who were the ones that would not believe, and which one would betray him.) ⁶⁵ And he added, "This is the very reason I told you that no one can come to me unless the Father makes it possible for him to do so."

⁶⁶ Because of this, many of his followers turned back and would not go with him any more. ⁶⁷ So Jesus said to the twelve disciples, "And you — would you like to leave also?" ⁶⁸ Simon Peter answered him: "Lord, to whom

would we go? You have the words that give eternal life. ⁶⁹ And now we believe and know that you are the Holy One from God." ⁷⁰ Jesus answered them, "Did I not choose the twelve of you? Yet one of you is a devil!" ⁷¹ He was talking about Judas, the son of Simon Iscariot. For Judas, even though he was one of the twelve disciples, was going to betray him.

Jesus and His Brothers

7 After this, Jesus travelled in Galilee; he did not want to travel in Judea, because the Jews there were wanting to kill him. ² The Jewish Feast of Tabernacles was near, ³ so Jesus' brothers said to him: "Leave this place and go

to Judea, so that your disciples will see the works you are doing. ⁴ No one hides what he is doing if he wants to be well known. Since you are doing these things, let the whole world know about you!" ⁵ (Not even his brothers believed in him.) ⁶ Jesus said to them: "The right time for me has not yet come. Any time is right for you. ⁷ The world cannot hate you, but it hates me, because I keep telling it that its ways are bad. ⁸ You go on to the feast. I am not going to this feast, because the right time has not come for me." ⁹ He told them this, and stayed on in Galilee.

Jesus at the Feast of Tabernacles

¹⁰ After his brothers went to the feast, Jesus also went; however, he did not go openly, but went secretly. ¹¹ The Jews were looking for him at the feast. "Where is he?" they asked. ¹² There was much whispering about him in the crowd. "He is a good man," some people said. "No," others said, "he fools the people." ¹³ But no one talked about him openly, because they were afraid of the Jews.

¹⁴ The feast was nearly half over when Jesus went to the Temple and began teaching. ¹⁵ The Jews, greatly surprised, said, "How does this man know so much when he has never been to school?" ¹⁶ Jesus answered: "What I teach is not mine, but comes from God, who sent me. ¹⁷ Whoever is willing to do what God wants will know whether what I teach comes from God or whether I speak on my own authority. ¹⁸ A person who speaks on his own is trying to gain glory for himself. He who wants glory for the one who sent him, however, is honest and there is nothing false in him. ¹⁹ Moses gave you the Law, did he not? But not one of you obeys the Law. Why are you trying to kill me?" ²⁰ The crowd answered, "You have a demon in you! Who is trying to kill you?" ²¹ Jesus answered: "I did one great work and you were all surprised. ²² Because Moses ordered you to circumcise your sons (although it was not Moses but your ancestors who started it), you will circumcise a boy on the Sabbath. ²³ If a boy is circumcised on the Sabbath so that Moses' Law will not be broken, why are you angry with me because I made a man completely well on the Sabbath? ²⁴ Stop judging by external standards, but judge by true standards."

Is He the Messiah?

25 Some of the people of Jerusalem said: "Isn't this the man they are trying to kill? 26 Look! He is talking in public, and nobody says anything against him! Can it be that the leaders really know that he is the Messiah? 27 But when the Messiah comes, no one will know where he is from. And we all know where this man comes from."

28 As Jesus taught in the Temple he said in a loud voice: "Do you really know me, and know where I am from? But I have not come on my own. He who sent me, however, is true. You do not know him, 29 but I know him, for I come from him and he sent me." 30 Then they tried to arrest him, but no one laid a hand on him, because his hour had not yet come. 31 But many in the crowd believed in him, and said, "When the Messiah comes, will he do more mighty works than this man has done?"

Guards Are Sent to Arrest Jesus

32 The Pharisees heard the crowd whispering these things about him, so they and the chief priests sent some guards to arrest Jesus. 33 Jesus said: "I shall be with you a little while longer, and then I shall go away to him who sent me. 34 You will look for me, but you will not find me; for where I shall be you cannot go." 35 The Jews said among themselves: "Where is he about to go so that we shall not find him? Will he go to the Greek cities where the Jews live, and teach the Greeks? 36 He says, 'You will look for me but you will not find me,' and, 'You cannot go where I shall be.' What does he mean?"

Streams of Living Water

37 The last day of the feast was the most important. On that day Jesus stood up and said in a loud voice: "Whoever is thirsty should come to me and drink. 38 As the scripture says, 'Whoever believes in me, streams of living water will pour out from his heart.'" 39 (Jesus said this about the Spirit which those who believed in him were about to receive. At that time the Spirit had not yet been given, because Jesus had not been raised to glory.)

Division among the People

40 Many of the people in the crowd heard him say this

and said, "This man is really the Prophet!" 41 Others said, "He is the Messiah!" But others said, "The Messiah will not come from Galilee! 42 The scripture says that the Messiah will be a descendant of David, and will be born in Bethlehem, the town where David lived." 43 So there was a division in the crowd because of him. 44 Some wanted to arrest him, but no one laid a hand on him.

The Unbelief of the Jewish Leaders

45 The guards went back to the chief priests and Pharisees, who asked them, "Why did you not bring him along?" 46 The guards answered, "Nobody has ever talked the way this man does!" 47 "Did he fool you, too?" the Pharisees asked them. 48 "Have you ever known one of our leaders or one Pharisee to believe in him? 49 This crowd does not know the Law of Moses, so they are under God's curse!" 50 Nicodemus was one of them; he was the one who had gone to see Jesus before. He said to them, 51 "According to our Law we cannot condemn a man before hearing him and finding out what he has done." 52 "Well," they answered, "are you also from Galilee? Study the Scriptures and you will learn that no prophet ever comes from Galilee."

The Woman Caught in Adultery

8 [Then everyone went home, but Jesus went to the Mount of Olives. 2 Early the next morning he went

back to the Temple. The whole crowd gathered around
him, and he sat down and began to teach them. ³ The
teachers of the Law and the Pharisees brought in a woman
who had been caught committing adultery, and made her
stand before them all. ⁴ "Teacher," they said to Jesus,
"this woman was caught in the very act of committing
adultery. ⁵ In our Law Moses gave a commandment that
such a woman must be stoned to death. Now, what do
you say?" ⁶ They said this to trap him, so they could
accuse him. But Jesus bent over and wrote on the ground
with his finger. ⁷ As they stood there asking questions,

Jesus straightened up and said to them, "Whichever one
of you has committed no sin may throw the first stone at
her." ⁸ Then he bent over again and wrote on the ground.
⁹ When they heard this they all left, one by one, the older
ones first. Jesus was left alone, with the woman still standing there. ¹⁰ He straightened up and said to her, "Where
are they, woman? Is there no one left to condemn you?"

[11] "No one, sir," she answered. "Well, then," Jesus said, "I do not condemn you either. You may leave, but do not sin again."]

Jesus the Light of the World

[12] Jesus spoke to them again: "I am the light of the world. Whoever follows me will have the light of life and will never walk in the darkness." [13] The Pharisees said to him, "Now you are testifying on your own behalf; what you say proves nothing." [14] "No," Jesus answered, "even if I do testify on my own behalf, what I say is true, because I know where I came from and where I am going. You do not know where I came from or where I am going. [15] You make judgments in a purely human way; I pass judgment on no one. [16] But if I were to pass judgment, my judging would be true, because I am not alone in this; the Father who sent me is with me. [17] It is written in your Law that when two witnesses agree, what they say is true. [18] I testify on my own behalf, and the Father who sent me also testifies on my behalf." [19] "Where is your father?" they asked him. "You know neither me nor my Father," Jesus answered. "If you knew me you would know my Father also."

[20] Jesus said all this as he taught in the Temple, in the room where the offering boxes were placed. And no one arrested him, because his hour had not come.

You Cannot Go Where I Am Going

[21] Jesus said to them again, "I will go away; you will look for me, but you will die in your sins. You cannot go where I am going." [22] So the Jews said, "He says, 'You cannot go where I am going.' Does this mean that he will kill himself?" [23] Jesus answered: "You come from here below, but I come from above. You come from this world, but I do not come from this world. [24] That is why I told you that you will die in your sins. And you will die in your sins if you do not believe that 'I Am Who I Am'." [25] "Who are you?" they asked him. Jesus answered: "What I have told you from the very beginning. [26] There are many things I have to say and judge about you. The one who sent me, however, is true, and I tell the world only what I have heard from him."

[27] They did not understand that he was talking to them

about the Father. ²⁸ So Jesus said to them: "When you lift up the Son of Man you will know that 'I Am Who I Am'; then you will know that I do nothing on my own, but say only what the Father has taught me. ²⁹ And he who sent me is with me; he has not left me alone, because I always do what pleases him." ³⁰ Many who heard Jesus say these things believed in him.

Free Men and Slaves

³¹ So Jesus said to the Jews who believed in him, "If you obey my teaching you are really my disciples; ³² you will know the truth, and the truth will make you free." ³³ "We are the descendants of Abraham," they answered, "and we have never been anybody's slaves. What do you mean, then, by saying, 'You will be made free'?" ³⁴ Jesus said to them: "I tell you the truth: everyone who sins is a slave of sin. ³⁵ A slave does not belong to the family always; but a son belongs there for ever. ³⁶ If the Son makes you free, then you will be really free. ³⁷ I know you are Abraham's descendants. Yet you are trying to kill me, because you will not accept my teaching. ³⁸ I talk about what my Father has shown me, but you do what your father has told you."

³⁹ They answered him, "Our father is Abraham." "If you really were Abraham's children," Jesus replied, "you would do the same works that he did. ⁴⁰ But all I have ever done is to tell you the truth I heard from God. Yet you are trying to kill me. Abraham did nothing like this! ⁴¹ You are doing what your father did." "We are not bastards," they answered. "We have the one Father, God himself." ⁴² Jesus said to them: "If God really were your father, you would love me; for I came from God and now I am here. I did not come on my own, but he sent me. ⁴³ Why do you not understand what I say? It is because you cannot bear to listen to my message. ⁴⁴ You are the children of your father, the Devil, and you want to follow your father's desires. From the very beginning he was a murderer. He has never been on the side of truth, because there is no truth in him. When he tells a lie he is only doing what is natural to him, because he is a liar and the father of all lies. ⁴⁵ I tell the truth, and that is why you do not believe me. ⁴⁶ Which one of you can prove that I am guilty of sin? If I tell the truth, then why do you

not believe me? ⁴⁷ He who comes from God listens to God's words. You, however, are not from God, and this is why you will not listen."

Jesus and Abraham

⁴⁸ The Jews replied to Jesus: "Were we not right in saying that you are a Samaritan and have a demon in you?" ⁴⁹ "I have no demon," Jesus answered. "I honour my Father, but you dishonour me. ⁵⁰ I am not seeking honour for myself. There is one who is seeking it and who judges in my favour. ⁵¹ I tell you the truth: whoever obeys my message will never die." ⁵² The Jews said to him: "Now we know for sure that you have a demon! Abraham died, and the prophets died, yet you say, 'Whoever obeys my message will never die.' ⁵³ Our father Abraham died; you do not claim to be greater than Abraham, do you? And the prophets also died. Who do you think you are?" ⁵⁴ Jesus answered: "If I were to honour myself, my own honour would be worth nothing. The one who honours me is my Father — the very one you say is your God. ⁵⁵ You have never known him, but I know him. If I were to say that I do not know him, I would be a liar, like you. But I do know him, and I obey his word. ⁵⁶ Your father Abraham rejoiced that he was to see my day; he saw it and was glad." ⁵⁷ The Jews said to him, "You are not even fifty years old — and have you seen Abraham?" ⁵⁸ "I tell you the truth," Jesus replied. "Before Abraham was born, 'I Am'." ⁵⁹ They picked up stones to throw at him; but Jesus hid himself and left the Temple.

Jesus Heals a Man Born Blind

9 As Jesus walked along he saw a man who had been born blind. ² His disciples asked him: "Teacher, whose sin was it that caused him to be born blind? His own or his parents' sin?" ³ Jesus answered: "His blindness has nothing to do with his sins or his parents' sins. He is blind so that God's power might be seen at work in him. ⁴ We must keep on doing the works of him who sent me, as long as it is day; the night is coming, when no one can work. ⁵ While I am in the world I am the light for the world." ⁶ After he said this, Jesus spat on the ground and made some mud with the spittle; he rubbed the mud on the man's eyes, ⁷ and told him, "Go wash your face in the

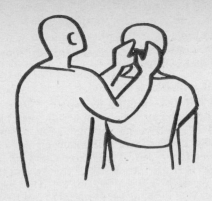

Pool of Siloam." (This name means "Sent.") So the man went, washed his face, and came back seeing.

⁸ His neighbours, then, and the people who had seen him begging before this, asked, "Isn't this the man who used to sit and beg?" ⁹ Some said, "He is the one," but others said, "No, he is not, he just looks like him." So the man himself said, "I am the man." ¹⁰ "How were your eyes opened?" they asked him. ¹¹ He answered, "The man named Jesus made some mud, rubbed it on my eyes, and told me, 'Go to Siloam and wash your face.' So I went, and as soon as I washed I could see." ¹² "Where is he?" they asked. "I do not know," he answered.

The Pharisees Investigate the Healing

¹³ Then they took the man who had been blind to the Pharisees. ¹⁴ The day that Jesus made the mud and opened the man's eyes was a Sabbath. ¹⁵ The Pharisees, then, asked the man again how he had received his sight. He told them, "He put some mud on my eyes, I washed my face, and now I can see." ¹⁶ Some of the Pharisees said, "The man who did this cannot be from God because he does not obey the Sabbath law." Others, however, said, "How could a man who is a sinner do such mighty works as these?" And there was a division among them.

¹⁷ So the Pharisees asked the man once more, "You say he opened your eyes — well, what do you say about him?" "He is a prophet," he answered. ¹⁸ The Jews, however, were not willing to believe that he had been blind and could now see, until they called the man's parents ¹⁹ and

asked them: "Is this your son? Do you say that he was born blind? Well, how is it that he can see now?" [20] His parents answered: "We know that he is our son, and we know that he was born blind. [21] But we do not know how it is that he is now able to see, nor do we know who opened his eyes. Ask him; he is old enough, and he can answer for himself!" [22] His parents said this because they were afraid of the Jews; for the Jews had already agreed that if anyone professed that Jesus was the Messiah he would be put out of the synagogue. [23] That is why his parents said, "He is old enough; ask him!"

[24] A second time they called back the man who had been born blind and said to him, "Promise before God that you will tell the truth! We know that this man is a sinner." [25] "I do not know if he is a sinner or not," the man replied. "One thing I do know: I was blind, and now I see." [26] "What did he do to you?" they asked. "How did he open your eyes?" [27] "I have already told you," he answered, "and you would not listen. Why do you want to hear it again? Maybe you, too, would like to be his disciples?" [28] They cursed him and said: "You are that fellow's disciple; we are Moses' disciples. [29] We know that God spoke to Moses; as for that fellow, we do not even know where he comes from!" [30] The man answered: "What a strange thing this is! You do not know where he comes from, but he opened my eyes! [31] We know that God does not listen to sinners; he does listen to people who respect him and do what he wants them to do. [32] Since the beginning of the world it has never been heard of that someone opened the eyes of a man born blind; [33] unless this man came from God, he would not be able to do a thing." [34] They answered back, "You were born and raised in sin — and you are trying to teach us?" And they threw him out of the synagogue.

Spiritual Blindness

[35] Jesus heard that they had thrown him out. He found him and said, "Do you believe in the Son of Man?" [36] The man answered, "Tell me who he is, sir, so I can believe in him!" [37] Jesus said to him, "You have already seen him, and he is the one who is talking with you now." [38] "I believe, Lord!" the man said, and knelt down before Jesus.

[39] Jesus said, "I came to this world to judge, so that the blind should see, and those who see should become blind." [40] Some Pharisees, who were there with him, heard him say this and asked him, "You don't mean that we are blind, too?" [41] Jesus answered, "If you were blind, then you would not be guilty; but since you say, 'We can see,' that means that you are still guilty."

The Parable of the Sheepfold

10 "I tell you the truth: the man who does not enter the sheepfold by the door, but climbs in some other way, is a thief and a robber. [2] The man who goes in by the door is the shepherd of the sheep. [3] The gatekeeper opens the gate for him; the sheep hear his voice as he calls his own sheep by name, and he leads them out. [4] When he has brought them out, he goes ahead of them, and the sheep follow him, because they know his voice. [5] They will

not follow someone else; instead, they will run away from him, because they do not know his voice."

[6] Jesus told them this parable, but they did not understand what he was telling them.

Jesus the Good Shepherd

[7] So Jesus said again: "I tell you the truth: I am the door for the sheep. [8] All others who came before me are thieves and robbers; but the sheep did not listen to them. [9] I am the door. Whoever comes in by me will be saved; he will come in and go out, and find pasture. [10] The thief comes only in order to steal, kill, and destroy. I have come in order that they might have life, life in all its fulness.

[11] "I am the good shepherd. The good shepherd is willing to die for the sheep. [12] The hired man, who is not a shepherd and does not own the sheep, leaves them and runs away when he sees a wolf coming; so the wolf

snatches the sheep and scatters them. ¹³ The hired man runs away because he is only a hired man and does not care for the sheep. ¹⁴⁻¹⁵ I am the good shepherd. As the Father knows me and I know the Father, in the same way I know my sheep and they know me. And I am willing to die for them. ¹⁶ There are other sheep that belong to me that are not in this sheepfold. I must bring them, too; they will listen to my voice, and they will become one flock with one shepherd.

¹⁷ "The Father loves me because I am willing to give up my life, in order that I may receive it back again. ¹⁸ No one takes my life away from me. I give it up of my own free will. I have the right to give it, and I have the right to take it back. This is what my Father has commanded me to do."

¹⁹ Again there was a division among the Jews because of these words. ²⁰ Many of them were saying, "He has a demon! He is crazy! Why do you listen to him?" ²¹ But others were saying, "A man with a demon could not talk like this! How could a demon open the eyes of blind men?"

Jesus Rejected by the Jews

²² The time came to celebrate the Feast of Dedication in Jerusalem; it was winter. ²³ Jesus was walking in Solomon's Porch in the Temple, ²⁴ when the Jews gathered around him and said, "How long are you going to keep us in suspense? Tell us the plain truth: are you the Messiah?" ²⁵ Jesus answered: "I have already told you, but you would not believe me. The works I do by my Father's authority speak on my behalf; ²⁶ but you will not believe because you are not my sheep. ²⁷ My sheep listen to my voice; I know them, and they follow me. ²⁸ I give them eternal life, and they shall never die; and no one can snatch them away from me. ²⁹ What my Father has given me is greater than all, and no one can snatch them away from the Father's care. ³⁰ The Father and I are one."

³¹ Then the Jews once more picked up stones to throw at him. ³² Jesus said to them, "I have done many good works before you which the Father gave me to do; for which one of these do you want to stone me?" ³³ The Jews answered back: "We do not want to stone you because of any good works, but because of the way in which

you insult God! You are only a man, but you are trying to make yourself God!" ³⁴ Jesus answered: "It is written in your own Law that God said, 'You are gods.' ³⁵ We know that what the scripture says is true for ever; and God called them gods, those people to whom his message was given. ³⁶ As for me, the Father chose me and sent me into the world. How, then, can you say that I insult God because I said that I am the Son of God? ³⁷ Do not believe me, then, if I am not doing my Father's works. ³⁸ But if I do them, even though you do not believe me, you should at least believe my works, in order that you may know once and for all that the Father is in me, and I am in the Father."

³⁹ Once more they tried to arrest him, but he slipped out of their hands.

⁴⁰ Jesus went back again across the Jordan river to the place where John had been baptizing, and stayed there. ⁴¹ Many people came to him. "John did no mighty works," they said, "but everything he said about this man was true." ⁴² And many people there believed in him.

The Death of Lazarus

11 A man named Lazarus, who lived in Bethany, became sick. Bethany was the town where Mary and her sister Martha lived. ² (This Mary was the one who poured the perfume on the Lord's feet and wiped them with her hair; it was her brother Lazarus who was sick.) ³ The sisters sent Jesus a message, "Lord, your dear friend is sick." ⁴ When Jesus heard it he said, "The final result of this sickness will not be the death of Lazarus; this has happened to bring glory to God, and will be the means by which the Son of God will receive glory."

⁵ Jesus loved Martha and her sister, and Lazarus. ⁶ When he received the news that Lazarus was sick, he stayed where he was for two more days. ⁷ Then he said to the disciples, "Let us go back to Judea." ⁸ "Teacher," the disciples answered, "just a short time ago the Jews wanted to stone you; and you plan to go back there?" ⁹ Jesus said: "A day has twelve hours, has it not? So if a man walks in broad daylight he does not stumble, because he sees the light of this world. ¹⁰ But if he walks during the night he stumbles, because there is no light in him." ¹¹ Jesus said this, and then added. "Our friend Lazarus has

fallen asleep, but I will go wake him up." 12 The disciples
answered, "If he is asleep, Lord, he will get well." 13 But
Jesus meant that Lazarus had died; they thought he meant
natural sleep. 14 So Jesus told them plainly, "Lazarus is
dead; 15 but for your sake I am glad that I was not with
him, so you will believe. Let us go to him." 16 Thomas
(called the Twin) said to his fellow disciples, "Let us all
go along with the Teacher, that we may die with him!"

Jesus the Resurrection and the Life

17 When Jesus arrived, he found that Lazarus had been
buried four days before. 18 Bethany was less than two
miles from Jerusalem, 19 and many Jews had come to see
Martha and Mary to comfort them about their brother's
death.

20 When Martha heard that Jesus was coming, she went
out to meet him; but Mary stayed at home. 21 Martha said
to Jesus, "If you had been here, Lord, my brother would
not have died! 22 But I know that even now God will give
you whatever you ask of him." 23 "Your brother will be
raised to life," Jesus told her. 24 "I know," she replied,
"that he will be raised to life on the last day." 25 Jesus
said to her: "I am the resurrection and the life. Whoever
believes in me will live, even though he dies; 26 and whoever lives and believes in me will never die. Do you believe this?" 27 "Yes, Lord!" she answered. "I do believe
that you are the Messiah, the Son of God, who was to
come into the world."

Jesus Weeps

28 After Martha said this she went back and called her
sister Mary privately. "The Teacher is here," she told her,
"and is asking for you." 29 When Mary heard this she got
up and hurried out to meet him. 30 (Jesus had not arrived in
the village yet, but was still in the place where Martha had
met him.) 31 The Jews who were in the house with Mary
comforting her followed her when they saw her get up and
hurry out. They thought that she was going to the grave,
to weep there.

32 When Mary arrived where Jesus was and saw him, she
fell at his feet. "Lord," she said, "if you had been here,
my brother would not have died!" 33 Jesus saw her weeping, and the Jews who had come with her weeping also;

his heart was touched, and he was deeply moved. [34] "Where have you buried him?" he asked them. "Come and see, Lord," they answered. [35] Jesus wept. [36] So the Jews said, "See how much he loved him!" [37] But some of them said, "He opened the blind man's eyes, didn't he? Could he not have kept Lazarus from dying?"

Lazarus Brought to Life

[38] Deeply moved once more, Jesus went to the tomb, which was a cave with a stone placed at the entrance. [39] "Take the stone away!" Jesus ordered. Martha, the dead man's sister, answered, "There will be a bad smell, Lord. He has been buried four days!" [40] Jesus said to her, "Didn't I tell you that you would see God's glory if you believed?" [41] They took the stone away. Jesus looked up and said: "I thank you, Father, that you listen to me. [42] I know that you always listen to me, but I say this because of the people here, so they will believe that you sent me." [43] After he had said this he called out in a loud

voice, "Lazarus, come out!" [44] The dead man came out, his hands and feet wrapped in grave cloths, and a cloth around his face. "Untie him," Jesus told them, "and let him go."

The Plot against Jesus
(Also Matt. 26.1–5; Mark 14.1–2; Luke 22.1–2)

[45] Many of the Jews who had come to visit Mary saw

what Jesus did, and believed in him. 46 But some of them returned to the Pharisees and told them what Jesus had done. 47 So the Pharisees and the chief priests met with the Council and said: "What shall we do? All the mighty works this man is doing! 48 If we let him go on in this way everyone will believe in him, and the Roman authorities will take action and destroy the Temple and our whole nation!" 49 One of them, named Caiaphas, who was High Priest that year, said: "You do not know a thing! 50 Don't you realize that it is better for you to have one man die for the people, instead of the whole nation being destroyed?" 51 (Actually, he did not say this of his own accord; rather, as he was High Priest that year, he was prophesying that Jesus was about to die for the Jewish people, 52 and not only for them, but also to bring together into one body all the scattered children of God.) 53 So from that day on the Jewish authorities made plans to kill Jesus. 54 Therefore Jesus did not travel openly in Judea, but left and went to a place near the desert, to a town named Ephraim, where he stayed with the disciples.

55 The Jewish Feast of Passover was near, and many people went up from the country to Jerusalem, to perform the ceremony of purification before the feast. 56 They were looking for Jesus, and as they gathered in the Temple they asked one another, "What do you think? Surely he will not come to the feast, will he?" 57 The chief priests and the Pharisees had given orders that if anyone knew where Jesus was he must report it, so they could arrest him.

Jesus Anointed at Bethany
(Also Matt. 26.6–13; Mark 14.3–9)

12 Six days before the Passover, Jesus went to Bethany, where Lazarus lived, the man Jesus had raised from death. 2 They had prepared a dinner for him there, and Martha helped serve it, while Lazarus sat at the table with Jesus. 3 Then Mary took a whole pint of a very expensive perfume made of nard, poured it on Jesus' feet, and wiped them with her hair. The sweet smell of the perfume filled the whole house. 4 One of Jesus' disciples, Judas Iscariot — the one who would betray him — said, 5 "Why wasn't this perfume sold for thirty pounds and the money given to the poor?" 6 He said this, not because he cared for

the poor, but because he was a thief; he carried the money bag and would help himself from it. [7] But Jesus said: "Leave her alone! Let her keep what she has for the day of my burial. [8] You will always have poor people with you, but I will not be with you always."

The Plot against Lazarus

[9] A large crowd of the Jews heard that Jesus was in Bethany, so they went there; they went, not only because of Jesus, but also to see Lazarus, whom Jesus had raised from death. [10] So the chief priests made plans to kill Lazarus too; [11] because on his account many Jews were leaving their leaders and believing in Jesus.

The Triumphant Entry into Jerusalem
(Also Matt. 21.1–11; Mark 11.1–11; Luke 19.28–40)

[12] The next day the large crowd that had come to the Passover Feast heard that Jesus was coming to Jerusalem. [13] So they took branches from palm trees and went out to meet him, shouting: "Praise God! God bless him who comes in the name of the Lord! God bless the King of Israel!" [14] Jesus found a donkey and sat on it, just as the scripture says:

[15] "Do not be afraid, city of Zion!
Now your King is coming to you,
Riding a young donkey."

[16] His disciples did not understand this at the time; but when Jesus had been raised to glory they remembered that the scripture said this, and that they had done this for him.

[17] The crowd that had been with Jesus when he called Lazarus out of the grave and raised him from death had reported what had happened. [18] That was why the crowd met him — because they heard that he had done this mighty work. [19] The Pharisees then said to each other, "You see, we are not succeeding at all! Look, the whole world is following him!"

Some Greeks Seek Jesus

[20] Some Greeks were among those who went to Jerusalem to worship during the feast. [21] They came to Philip (he was from Bethsaida, in Galilee) and said, "Sir, we want to see Jesus." [22] Philip went and told Andrew,

and the two of them went and told Jesus. [23] Jesus answered them: "The hour has now come for the Son of Man to be given great glory. [24] I tell you the truth: a grain of wheat is no more than a single grain unless it is dropped into the ground and dies. If it does die, then it produces many grains. [25] Whoever loves his own life will lose it; whoever hates his own life in this world will keep it for life eternal. [26] Whoever wants to serve me must follow me, so that my servant will be with me where I am. My Father will honour him who serves me."

Jesus Speaks about His Death

[27] "Now my heart is troubled — and what shall I say? Shall I say, 'Father, do not let this hour come upon me'? But that is why I came, to go through this hour of suffering. [28] O Father, bring glory to your name!" Then a voice spoke from heaven, "I have brought glory to it, and I will do so again."

[29] The crowd standing there heard the voice and said, "It thundered!" Others said, "An angel spoke to him!" [30] But Jesus said to them: "It was not for my sake that this voice spoke, but for yours. [31] Now is the time for the world to be judged; now the ruler of this world will be overthrown. [32] When I am lifted up from the earth, I will draw all men to me." [33] (In saying this he indicated the kind of death he was going to suffer.) [34] The crowd answered back: "Our Law tells us that the Messiah will live for ever. How, then, can you say that the Son of Man must be lifted up? Who is this Son of Man?" [35] Jesus answered: "The light will be among you a little longer. Live your lives while you have the light, so the darkness will not come upon you; because the one who lives in the dark does not know where he is going. [36] Believe in the light, then, while you have it, so that you will be the people of the light."

The Unbelief of the Jews

After Jesus said this he went off and hid himself from them. [37] Even though he had done all these mighty works before their very eyes they did not believe in him, [38] so that what the prophet Isaiah had said might come true:

"Lord, who believed the message we told?
To whom did the Lord show his power?"

[39] For this reason they were not able to believe, because Isaiah also said:

[40] "God has blinded their eyes,
He has closed their minds,
So that their eyes would not see,
Their minds would not understand,
And they would not turn to me
For me to heal them."

[41] Isaiah said this because he saw Jesus' glory, and spoke about him.

[42] Even then, many Jewish leaders believed in Jesus; but because of the Pharisees they did not talk about it openly, so as not to be put out of the synagogue. [43] They loved the approval of men rather than the approval of God.

Judgment by Jesus' Word

[44] Jesus spoke in a loud voice: "Whoever believes in me, believes not only in me but also in him who sent me. [45] Whoever sees me, also sees him who sent me. [46] I have come into the world as light, that everyone who believes in me should not remain in the darkness. [47] Whoever hears my message and does not obey it, I will not judge him. I came, not to judge the world, but to save it. [48] Whoever rejects me and does not accept my message, has one who will judge him. The word I have spoken will be his judge on the last day! [49] Yes, because I have not spoken on my own, but the Father who sent me has commanded me what I must say and speak. [50] And I know that his command brings eternal life. What I say, then, is what the Father has told me to say."

Jesus Washes His Disciples' Feet

13 It was now the day before the Feast of Passover. Jesus knew that his hour had come for him to leave this world and go to the Father. He had always loved those who were his own in the world, and he loved them to the very end.

[2] Jesus and his disciples were at supper. The Devil had already decided that Judas, the son of Simon Iscariot, would betray Jesus. [3] Jesus knew that the Father had given him complete power; he knew that he had come from God and was going to God. [4] So Jesus rose from the

table, took off his outer garment, and tied a towel round his waist. [5] Then he poured some water into a washbasin and began to wash the disciples' feet and dry them with the towel round his waist. [6] He came to Simon Peter, who said to him, "Are you going to wash my feet, Lord?" [7] Jesus answered him, "You do not know now what I am doing, but you will know later." [8] Peter declared, "You will never, at any time, wash my feet!" "If I do not wash your feet," Jesus answered, "you will no longer be my disciple." [9] Simon Peter answered, "Lord, do not wash only my feet, then! Wash my hands and head, too!" [10] Jesus said: "Whoever has taken a bath is completely clean and does not have to wash himself, except for his feet. All of you are clean — all except one." [11] (Jesus already knew who was going to betray him; that is why he said, "All of you, except one, are clean.")

[12] After he had washed their feet, Jesus put his outer garment back on and returned to his place at the table. "Do you understand what I have just done to you?" he asked. [13] "You call me Teacher and Lord, and it is right that you do so, because I am. [14] I am your Lord and Teacher, and I have just washed your feet. You, then, should wash each other's feet. [15] I have set an example for you, so that you will do just what I have done for you. [16] I tell you the truth: no slave is greater than his master; no messenger is greater than the one who sent him. [17] Now you know this truth; how happy you will be if you put it into practice!

[18] "I am not talking about all of you; I know those I have chosen. But the scripture must come true that says, 'The man who ate my food turned against me.' [19] I tell you this now before it happens, so that when it does happen you will believe that 'I Am Who I Am'. [20] I tell you the truth: whoever receives anyone I send, receives me also; and whoever receives me, receives him who sent me."

Jesus Predicts His Betrayal
(Also Matt. 26.20–25; Mark 14.17–21; Luke 22.21–23)

21 After Jesus said this, he was deeply troubled, and declared openly: "I tell you the truth: one of you is going
to betray me." 22 The disciples looked at one another,
completely puzzled about whom he meant. 23 One of the

disciples, whom Jesus loved, was sitting next to Jesus.
24 Simon Peter motioned to him and said, "Ask him who
it is that he is talking about." 25 So that disciple moved
closer to Jesus' side and asked, "Who is it, Lord?" 26 Jesus
answered, "I will dip the bread in the sauce and give it
to him; he is the man." So he took a piece of bread,
dipped it, and gave it to Judas, the son of Simon Iscariot.
27 As soon as Judas took the bread, Satan went into him.
Jesus said to him, "Hurry and do what you must!"
28 (None of those at the table understood what Jesus said
to him. 29 Since Judas was in charge of the money bag,
some of the disciples thought that Jesus had told him to go
to buy what they needed for the feast, or else that he had
told him to give something to the poor.) 30 Judas accepted
the bread and went out at once. It was night.

The New Commandment

31 After Judas had left, Jesus said: "Now the Son of

Man's glory is revealed; now God's glory is revealed through him. [32] And if God's glory is revealed through him, then God himself will reveal the glory of the Son of Man, and he will do so at once. [33] My children, I shall not be with you very much longer. You will look for me; but I tell you now what I told the Jews, 'You cannot go where I am going.' [34] A new commandment I give you: love one another. As I have loved you, so you must love one another. [35] If you have love for one another, then all will know that you are my disciples."

Jesus Predicts Peter's Denial
(Also Matt. 26.31–35; Mark 14.27–31; Luke 22.31–34)

[36] "Where are you going, Lord?" Simon Peter asked him. "You cannot follow me now where I am going," answered Jesus; "but later you will follow me." [37] "Lord, why can't I follow you now?" asked Peter. "I am ready to die for you!" [38] Jesus answered: "Are you really ready to die for me? I tell you the truth: before the rooster crows you will say three times that you do not know me."

Jesus the Way to the Father

14 "Do not be worried and upset," Jesus told them. "Believe in God, and believe also in me. [2] There are many rooms in my Father's house, and I am going to prepare a place for you. I would not tell you this if it were not so. [3] And after I go and prepare a place for you, I will come back and take you to myself, so that you will be where I am. [4] You know how to get to the place where I am going." [5] Thomas said to him, "Lord, we do not know where you are going; how can we know the way to get there?" [6] Jesus answered him: "I am the way, I am the truth, I am the life; no one goes to the Father except by me. [7] Now that you have known me," he said to them, "you will know my Father also; and from now on you do know him, and you have seen him."

[8] Philip said to him, "Lord, show us the Father; that is all we need." [9] Jesus answered: "For a long time I have been with you all; yet you do not know me, Philip? Whoever has seen me has seen the Father. Why, then, do you say, 'Show us the Father'? [10] Do you not believe, Philip, that I am in the Father and the Father is in me? The words that I have spoken to you," Jesus said to his

disciples, "do not come from me. The Father, who remains in me, does his own works. [11] Believe me that I am in the Father and the Father is in me. If not, believe because of these works. [12] I tell you the truth: whoever believes in me will do the works I do — yes, he will do even greater ones, for I am going to the Father. [13] And I will do whatever you ask for in my name, so that the Father's glory will be shown through the Son. [14] If you ask me for anything in my name, I will do it."

The Promise of the Holy Spirit

[15] "If you love me, you will obey my commandments. [16] I will ask the Father, and he will give you another Helper, the Spirit of truth, to stay with you for ever. [17] The world cannot receive him, because it cannot see him or know him. But you know him, for he remains with you and lives in you.

[18] "I will not leave you alone; I will come back to you. [19] In a little while the world will see me no more, but you will see me; and because I live, you also will live. [20] When that day comes, you will know that I am in my Father, and that you are in me, just as I am in you.

[21] "Whoever accepts my commandments and obeys them, he is the one who loves me. My Father will love him who loves me; I too will love him and reveal myself to him." [22] Judas (not Judas Iscariot) said, "Lord, how can it be that you will reveal yourself to us and not to the world?" [23] Jesus answered him: "Whoever loves me will obey my message. My Father will love him, and my Father and I will come to him and live with him. [24] Whoever does not love me does not obey my words. The message you have heard is not mine, but comes from the Father, who sent me.

[25] "I have told you this while I am still with you. [26] The Helper, the Holy Spirit whom the Father will send in my name, will teach you everything, and make you remember all that I have told you.

[27] "Peace I leave with you; my own peace I give you. I do not give it to you as the world does. Do not be worried and upset; do not be afraid. [28] You heard me say to you, 'I am leaving, but I will come back to you.' If you loved me, you would be glad that I am going to the Father, because he is greater than I. [29] I have told you this now,

before it all happens, so that when it does happen you will believe. [30] I cannot talk with you much longer, for the ruler of this world is coming. He has no power over me, [31] but the world must know that I love the Father; that is why I do everything as he commands me.

"Rise, let us go from this place."

Jesus the Real Vine

15 "I am the real vine, and my Father is the gardener. [2] He breaks off every branch in me that does not bear fruit, and prunes every branch that does bear fruit, so that it will be clean and bear more fruit. [3] You have been made clean already by the message I have spoken to you. [4] Remain in union with me, and I will remain in union with you. Unless you remain in me you cannot bear fruit, just as a branch cannot bear fruit unless it remains in the vine.

[5] "I am the vine, you are the branches. Whoever remains in me, and I in him, will bear much fruit; for you can do nothing without me. [6] Whoever does not remain in me is thrown out, like a branch, and dries up; such branches are gathered up and thrown into the fire, where they are burned. [7] If you remain in me, and my words remain in you, then you will ask for anything you wish, and you shall have it. [8] This is how my Father's glory is shown: by your bearing much fruit; and in this way you become my disciples. [9] I love you just as the Father loves me; remain in my love. [10] If you obey my commands, you will remain in my love, in the same way that I have obeyed my Father's commands and remain in his love.

[11] "I have told you this so that my joy may be in you, and that your joy may be complete. [12] This is my commandment: love one another, just as I love you. [13] The greatest love a man can have for his friends is to give his life for them. [14] And you are my friends, if you do what I command. [15] I do not call you servants any longer, because a servant does not know what his master is doing. Instead, I call you friends, because I have told you everything I heard from my Father. [16] You did not choose me; I chose you, and appointed you to go and bear much fruit, the kind of fruit that endures. And the Father will give you whatever you ask of him in my name. [17] This, then, is what I command you: love one another."

The World's Hatred

18 "If the world hates you, you must remember that it has hated me first. 19 If you belonged to the world, then the world would love you as its own. But I chose you from this world, and you do not belong to it; this is why

the world hates you. 20 Remember what I told you: 'No slave is greater than his master.' If they persecuted me, they will persecute you too; if they obeyed my message, they will obey yours too. 21 But they will do all this to you because you are mine; for they do not know him who sent me. 22 They would not have been guilty of sin if I had not come and spoken to them; as it is, they no longer have any excuse for their sin. 23 Whoever hates me hates my Father also. 24 They would not have been guilty of sin if I had not done the works among them that no one else ever did; as it is, they have seen what I did and they hate both me and my Father. 25 This must be, however, so that what is written in their Law may come true, 'They hated me for no reason at all.'

26 "The Helper will come — the Spirit of truth, who comes from the Father. I will send him from the Father, and he will speak about me. 27 And you, too, will speak

about me, for you have been with me from the very beginning.

16 "I have told you this so that you will not fall away. ² They will put you out of their synagogues. And the time will come when anyone who kills you will think that by doing this he is serving God. ³ They will do these things to you because they have not known either the Father or me. ⁴ But I have told you this, so that when the time comes for them to do these things, you will remember that I told you."

The Work of the Holy Spirit

"I did not tell you these things at the beginning, because I was with you. ⁵ But now I am going to him who sent me; but none of you asks me, 'Where are you going?' ⁶ And now that I have told you, sadness has filled your hearts. ⁷ But I tell you the truth: it is better for you that I go away, because if I do not go, the Helper will not come to you. But if I do go away, then I will send him to you. ⁸ And when he comes he will prove to the people of the world that they are wrong about sin, and about what is right, and about God's judgment. ⁹ They are wrong about sin, because they do not believe in me; ¹⁰ about what is right, because I am going to the Father and you will not see me any more; ¹¹ about judgment, because the ruler of this world has already been judged.

¹² "I have much more to tell you, but now it would be too much for you to bear. ¹³ But when the Spirit of truth comes, he will lead you into all the truth. He will not speak on his own, but he will tell you what he hears, and will speak of things to come. ¹⁴ He will give me glory, for he will take what I have to say and tell it to you. ¹⁵ All that my Father has is mine; that is why I said that the Spirit will take what I give him and tell it to you."

Sadness and Gladness

¹⁶ "In a little while you will not see me any more; and then a little while later you will see me." ¹⁷ Some of his disciples said to the others: "What does this mean? He tells us, 'In a little while you will not see me, and then a little while later you will see me'; and he also says, 'It is because I am going to the Father.' ¹⁸ What does this 'a little while' mean?" they asked. "We do not know what he

is talking about!" ¹⁹ Jesus knew that they wanted to ask him, so he said to them: "I said, 'In a little while you will not see me, and then a little while later you will see me.' Is this what you are asking about among yourselves? ²⁰ I tell you the truth: you will cry and weep, but the world will be glad; you will be sad, but your sadness will turn into gladness. ²¹ When a woman is about to give birth to a child she is sad, because her hour of suffering has come; but when the child is born she forgets her suffering, because she is happy that a baby has been born into the world. ²² That is the way it is with you: now you are sad, but I will see you again, and your hearts will be filled with gladness, the kind of gladness that no one can take away from you.

²³ "When that day comes you will not ask me for a thing. I tell you the truth: the Father will give you anything you ask of him in my name. ²⁴ Until now you have not asked for anything in my name; ask and you will receive, so that your happiness may be complete."

Victory over the World

²⁵ "I have told you these things by means of parables. But the time will come when I will use parables no more, but I will speak to you in plain words about the Father. ²⁶ When that day comes you will ask him in my name; and I do not say that I will ask him on your behalf, ²⁷ for the Father himself loves you. He loves you because you love me and have believed that I came from God. ²⁸ I did come from the Father and I came into the world; and now I am leaving the world and going to the Father."

²⁹ Then his disciples said to him: "Look, you are speaking very plainly now, without using parables. ³⁰ We know now that you know everything; you do not need someone to ask you questions. This makes us believe that you came from God." ³¹ Jesus answered them: "Do you believe now? ³² The time is coming, and is already here, when all of you will be scattered, each one to his own home, and I will be left all alone. But I am not really alone, because the Father is with me. ³³ I have told you this so that you will have peace through your union with me. The world will make you suffer. But be brave! I have defeated the world!"

Jesus Prays for His Disciples

17 After Jesus finished saying this, he looked up to heaven and said: "Father, the hour has come.

Give glory to your Son, that the Son may give glory to you. ² For you gave him authority over all men, so that he might give eternal life to all those you gave him. ³ And this is eternal life: for men to know you, the only true God, and to know Jesus Christ, whom you sent. ⁴ I showed your glory on earth; I finished the work you gave me to do. ⁵ O Father! Give me glory in your presence now, the same glory I had with you before the world was made.

⁶ "I have made you known to the men you gave me out of the world. They belonged to you, and you gave them to me. They have obeyed your word, ⁷ and now they know that everything you gave me comes from you. ⁸ For I gave them the message that you gave me, and they received it; they know that it is true that I came from you, and they believe that you sent me.

⁹ "I pray for them. I do not pray for the world, but for the men you gave me, because they belong to you. ¹⁰ All I have is yours, and all you have is mine; and my glory is shown through them. ¹¹ And now I am coming to you; I am no longer in the world, but they are in the world. O holy Father! Keep them safe by the power of your name, the name you gave me, so they may be one just as you and I are one. ¹² While I was with them I kept them safe by the power of your name, the name you gave me. I protected them, and not one of them was lost, except the man who was bound to be lost — that the scripture might

come true. [13] And now I am coming to you, and I say these things in the world so that they might have my joy in their hearts, in all its fulness. [14] I gave them your message and the world hated them, because they do not belong to the world, just as I do not belong to the world. [15] I do not ask you to take them out of the world, but I do ask you to keep them safe from the Evil One. [16] Just as I do not belong to the world, they do not belong to the world. [17] Make them your own, by means of the truth; your word is truth. [18] I sent them into the world just as you sent me into the world. [19] And for their sake I give myself to you, in order that they, too, may truly belong to you.

[20] "I do not pray only for them, but also for those who believe in me because of their message. [21] I pray that they may all be one. O Father! May they be in us, just as you are in me and I am in you. May they be one, so that the world will believe that you sent me. [22] I gave them the same glory you gave me, so that they may be one, just as you and I are one: [23] I in them and you in me, so they may be completely one, in order that the world may know that you sent me and that you love them as you love me.

[24] "O Father! You have given them to me, and I want them to be with me where I am, so they may see my glory, the glory you gave me; for you loved me before the world was made. [25] O righteous Father! The world does not know you, but I know you, and these know that you sent me. [26] I made you known to them and I will continue to do so, in order that the love you have for me may be in them, and I may be in them."

The Arrest of Jesus
(Also Matt. 26.47-56; Mark 14.43-50; Luke 22.47-53)

18 After Jesus had said this prayer he left with his disciples and went across the brook Kidron. There was a garden in that place, and Jesus and his disciples went in. [2] Judas, the traitor, knew where it was, because many times Jesus had met there with his disciples. [3] So Judas went to the garden, taking with him a group of soldiers and some Temple guards sent by the chief priests and the Pharisees; they were armed and carried lanterns and torches. [4] Jesus knew everything that was going to happen to him; so he stepped forward and said to them, "Who is it

you are looking for?" ⁵ "Jesus of Nazareth," they answered. "I am he," he said.

Judas, the traitor, was standing there with them. ⁶ When Jesus said to them, "I am he," they moved back and fell to the ground. ⁷ Jesus asked them again, "Who is it you are

looking for?" "Jesus of Nazareth," they said. ⁸ "I have already told you that I am he," Jesus said. "If, then, you are looking for me, let these others go." ⁹ (He said this so that what he had said might come true: "Not a single one was lost, Father, of all those you gave me.") ¹⁰ Simon Peter had a sword; he drew it and struck the High Priest's slave, cutting off his right ear. The name of the slave was Malchus. ¹¹ Jesus said to Peter, "Put your sword back in its place! Do you think that I will not drink the cup of suffering my Father has given me?"

Jesus before Annas

¹² The group of soldiers with their commanding officer and the Jewish guards arrested Jesus, tied him up, ¹³ and took him first to Annas. He was the father-in-law of Caiaphas, who was High Priest that year. ¹⁴ It was Caiaphas who had advised the Jews that it was better that one man die for all the people.

Peter Denies Jesus
(Also Matt. 26.69–70; Mark 14.66–68; Luke 22.55–57)

¹⁵ Simon Peter and another disciple followed Jesus. That other disciple was well known to the High Priest, so he

went with Jesus into the courtyard of the High Priest's house. ¹⁶ Peter stayed outside by the gate. The other disciple, who was well known to the High Priest, went back out, spoke to the girl at the gate and brought Peter inside. ¹⁷ The girl at the gate said to Peter, "Aren't you one of the disciples of that man?" "No, I am not," answered Peter.

¹⁸ It was cold, so the servants and guards had built a charcoal fire and were standing around it, warming themselves. Peter went over and stood with them, warming himself.

The High Priest Questions Jesus
(Also Matt. 26.59–66; Mark 14.55–64; Luke 22.66–71)

¹⁹ The High Priest questioned Jesus about his disciples and about his teaching. ²⁰ Jesus answered: "I have always spoken publicly to everyone; all my teaching was done in the synagogues and in the Temple, where all the Jews come together. I have never said anything in secret. ²¹ Why, then, do you question me? Question the people who heard me. Ask them what I told them — they know what I said." ²² When Jesus said this, one of the guards there slapped him and said, "How dare you talk like this to the High Priest!" ²³ Jesus answered him: "If I have said something wrong, tell everyone here what it was. But if I am right in what I have said, why do you hit me?"

²⁴ So Annas sent him, still tied up, to Caiaphas the High Priest.

Peter Denies Jesus again
(Also Matt. 26.71–75; Mark 14.69–72; Luke 22.58–62)

²⁵ Peter was still standing there keeping himself warm. So the others said to him, "Aren't you one of the disciples of that man?" But Peter denied it. "No, I am not," he said. ²⁶ One of the High Priest's slaves, a relative of the man whose ear Peter had cut off, spoke up. "Didn't I see you with him in the garden?" he asked. ²⁷ Again Peter said "No" — and at once a rooster crowed.

Jesus before Pilate
(Also Matt. 27.1–2, 11–14; Mark 15.1–5; Luke 23.1–5)

²⁸ They took Jesus from Caiaphas' house to the Governor's palace. It was early in the morning. The Jews did

not go inside the palace because they wanted to keep themselves ritually clean, in order to be able to eat the
Passover meal. ²⁹ So Pilate went outside to meet them and
said, "What do you accuse this man of?" ³⁰ Their answer
was, "We would not have brought him to you if he had
not committed a crime." ³¹ Pilate said to them, "You
yourselves take him and try him according to your own
law." The Jews replied, "We are not allowed to put anyone to death." ³² (This happened to make come true what
Jesus had said when he indicated the kind of death he
would die.) ³³ Pilate went back into the palace and called
Jesus. "Are you the king of the Jews?" he asked him.
³⁴ Jesus answered, "Does this question come from you or
have others told you about me?" ³⁵ Pilate replied: "Do
you think I am a Jew? It was your own people and their
chief priests who handed you over to me. What have you
done?" ³⁶ Jesus said: "My kingdom does not belong to
this world; if my kingdom belonged to this world, my followers would fight to keep me from being handed over to
the Jews. No, my kingdom does not belong here!" ³⁷ So
Pilate asked him, "Are you a king, then?" Jesus answered:
"You say that I am a king. I was born and came into the
world for this one purpose, to speak about the truth. Whoever belongs to the truth listens to me." ³⁸ "And what is
truth?" Pilate asked.

Jesus Sentenced to Death
(Also Matt. 27.15–31; Mark 15.6–20; Luke 23.13–25)

Then Pilate went back outside to the Jews and said to

them: "I cannot find any reason to condemn him. ³⁹ But according to the custom you have, I always set free a prisoner for you during the Passover. Do you want me to set the king of the Jews free for you?" ⁴⁰ They answered him with a shout, "No, not him! We want Barabbas!" (Barabbas was a bandit.)

19 Then Pilate took Jesus and had him whipped. ² The soldiers made a crown of thorny branches and put it on his head; they put a purple robe on him, ³ and came to him and said, "Long live the King of the Jews!" And they went up and slapped him.

⁴ Pilate went back out once more and said to the crowd, "Look, I will bring him out here to you, to let you see that I cannot find any reason to condemn him." ⁵ So Jesus went outside, wearing the crown of thorns and the purple robe. Pilate said to them, "Look! Here is the man!" ⁶ When the chief priests and the guards saw him they shouted, "Nail him to the cross! Nail him to the cross!" Pilate said to them, "You take him, then, and nail him to the cross. I find no reason to condemn him." ⁷ The Jews answered back, "We have a law that says he ought to die, because he claimed to be the Son of God."

⁸ When Pilate heard them say this, he was even more afraid. ⁹ He went back into the palace and said to Jesus, "Where do you come from?" But Jesus gave him no answer. ¹⁰ Pilate said to him, "You will not speak to me? Remember, I have the authority to set you free, and also the authority to have you nailed to the cross." ¹¹ Jesus answered, "You have authority over me only because it was given to you by God. So the man who handed me over to you is guilty of a worse sin." ¹² When Pilate heard this he was all the more anxious to set him free. But the Jews shouted back, "If you set him free that means you are not the Emperor's friend! Anyone who claims to be a king is the Emperor's enemy!" ¹³ When Pilate heard these words, he took Jesus outside and sat down on the judge's seat in the place called "The Stone Pavement." (In Hebrew the name is "Gabbatha.")

¹⁴ It was then almost noon of the day before the Passover. Pilate said to the Jews, "Here is your king!" ¹⁵ They shouted back, "Kill him! Kill him! Nail him to the cross!" Pilate asked them, "Do you want me to nail your king to the cross?" The chief priests answered, "The only king we have is the Emperor!" ¹⁶ Then Pilate handed Jesus over to them to be nailed to the cross.

Jesus Nailed to the Cross
(Also Matt. 27.32–44; Mark 15.21–32; Luke 23.26–43)

So they took charge of Jesus. ¹⁷ He went out, carrying his own cross, and came to "The Place of the Skull," as it is called. (In Hebrew it is called "Golgotha.") ¹⁸ There they nailed him to the cross; they also nailed two other men to crosses, one on each side, with Jesus between them.

¹⁹ Pilate wrote a notice and had it put on the cross. "Jesus of Nazareth, the King of the Jews," is what he wrote. ²⁰ Many Jews read this, because the place where Jesus was nailed to the cross was not far from the city. The notice was written in Hebrew, Latin, and Greek. ²¹ The Jewish chief priests said to Pilate, "Do not write 'The King of the Jews,' but rather, 'This man said, I am the King of the Jews.' " ²² Pilate answered, "What I have written stays written."

²³ After the soldiers had nailed Jesus to the cross, they took his clothes and divided them into four parts, one part for each soldier. They also took the robe, which was made of one piece of woven cloth, without any seams in it. ²⁴ The soldiers said to each other, "Let us not tear it; let us throw dice to see who will get it." This happened to make the scripture come true:

"They divided my clothes among themselves,
They gambled for my robe."

So the soldiers did this.

²⁵ Standing close to Jesus' cross were his mother, his mother's sister, Mary the wife of Clopas, and Mary Magdalene. ²⁶ Jesus saw his mother and the disciple he loved standing there; so he said to his mother, "Woman, here is your son." ²⁷ Then he said to the disciple, "Here is your

mother." And from that time the disciple took her to live in his home.

The Death of Jesus
(Also Matt. 27.45–56; Mark 15.33–41; Luke 23.44–49)

28 Jesus knew that by now everything had been completed; and in order to make the scripture come true he said, "I am thirsty." 29 A bowl was there, full of cheap wine; they soaked a sponge in the wine, put it on a branch of hyssop, and lifted it up to his lips. 30 Jesus took the wine and said, "It is finished!" Then he bowed his head and died.

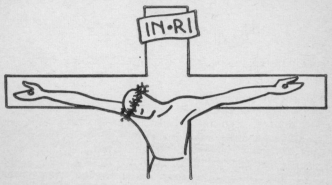

Jesus' Side Pierced

31 Then the Jews asked Pilate to allow them to break the legs of the men who had been put to death, and take them down from the crosses. They did this because it was Friday, and they did not want the bodies to stay on the crosses on the Sabbath day, since the coming Sabbath was especially holy. 32 So the soldiers went and broke the legs of the first man and then of the other man who had been put to death with Jesus. 33 But when they came to Jesus they saw that he was already dead, so they did not break his legs. 34 One of the soldiers, however, plunged his spear into Jesus' side, and at once blood and water poured out. 35 The one who saw this happen has spoken of it. We know that what he said is true, and he also knows that he speaks the truth, so that you also may believe. 36 This was done to make the scripture come true, "Not one of his

bones will be broken." ³⁷ And there is another scripture that says, "People will look at him whom they pierced."

The Burial of Jesus
(Also Matt. 27.57–61; Mark 15.42–47; Luke 23.50–56)

³⁸ After this, Joseph, who was from the town of Arimathea, asked Pilate if he could take Jesus' body. (Joseph was a follower of Jesus, but in secret, because he was afraid of the Jews.) Pilate told him he could have the body, so Joseph went and took it away. ³⁹ Nicodemus, who at first had gone to see Jesus at night, went with Joseph, taking with him about one hundred pounds of spices, a mixture of myrrh and aloes. ⁴⁰ The two men took Jesus' body and wrapped it in linen cloths with the spices; for this is how the Jews prepare a body for burial. ⁴¹ There was a garden in the place where Jesus had been put to death, and in it there was a new tomb where no one had ever been laid. ⁴² Since it was the day before the Jewish Sabbath, and because the tomb was close by, they laid Jesus there.

The Empty Tomb
(Also Matt. 28.1–8; Mark 16.1–8; Luke 24.1–12)

20 Early on Sunday morning, while it was still dark, Mary Magdalene went to the tomb and saw that the stone had been taken away from the entrance. ² She ran and went to Simon Peter and the other disciple, whom

Jesus loved, and told them, "They have taken the Lord from the tomb and we don't know where they have put him!" ³ Then Peter and the other disciple left and went to the tomb. ⁴ The two of them were running, but the other disciple ran faster than Peter and reached the tomb first. ⁵ He bent over and saw the linen cloths, but he did not go in. ⁶ Behind him came Simon Peter, and he went straight into the tomb. He saw the linen cloths lying there ⁷ and the cloth which had been around Jesus' head. It was not lying with the linen cloths but was rolled up by itself. ⁸ Then the other disciple, who had reached the tomb first, also went in; he saw and believed. ⁹ (They still did not understand the scripture which said that he must be raised from death.) ¹⁰ Then the disciples went back home.

Jesus Appears to Mary Magdalene
(Also Matt. 28.9–10; Mark 16.9–11)

¹¹ Mary stood crying outside the tomb. Still crying, she bent over and looked in the tomb, ¹² and saw two angels there, dressed in white, sitting where the body of Jesus had been, one at the head, the other at the feet. ¹³ "Woman, why are you crying?" they asked her. She answered, "They have taken my Lord away, and I do not know where they have put him!" ¹⁴ When she had said this, she turned round and saw Jesus standing there; but she did not know that it was Jesus. ¹⁵ "Woman, why are you crying?" Jesus asked her. "Who is it that you are looking for?" She thought he was the gardener, so she said to him, "If you took him away, sir, tell me where you have put him, and I will go and get him." ¹⁶ Jesus said to her, "Mary!" She turned toward him and said in Hebrew, "Rabboni!" (This means "Teacher.") ¹⁷ "Do not hold on to me," Jesus told her, "because I have not yet gone back up to the Father. But go to my brothers and tell them for me, 'I go back up to him who is my Father and your Father, my God and your God.'" ¹⁸ So Mary Magdalene told the disciples that she had seen the Lord, and that he had told her this.

Jesus Appears to His Disciples
(Also Matt. 28.16–20; Mark 16.14–18; Luke 24.36–49)

¹⁹ It was late that Sunday evening, and the disciples were gathered together behind locked doors, because they were

afraid of the Jews. Then Jesus came and stood among them. "Peace be with you," he said. ²⁰ After saying this, he showed them his hands and his side. The disciples were filled with joy at seeing the Lord. ²¹ Then Jesus said to them again, "Peace be with you. As the Father sent me, so I send you." ²² He said this, and then he breathed on them and said, "Receive the Holy Spirit. ²³ If you forgive men's sins, then they are forgiven; if you do not forgive them, then they are not forgiven."

Jesus and Thomas

²⁴ One of the disciples, Thomas (called the Twin), was not with them when Jesus came. ²⁵ So the other disciples told him, "We saw the Lord!" Thomas said to them, "If I do not see the scars of the nails in his hands, and put my finger where the nails were, and my hand in his side, I will not believe."

²⁶ A week later the disciples were together indoors again, and Thomas was with them. The doors were locked, but Jesus came and stood among them and said, "Peace be with you." ²⁷ Then he said to Thomas, "Put your finger here, and look at my hands; then stretch out your hand and put it in my side. Stop your doubting and believe!" ²⁸ Thomas answered him, "My Lord and my God!" ²⁹ Jesus said to him, "Do you believe because you see me? How happy are those who believe without seeing me!"

The Purpose of this Book

³⁰ Jesus did many other mighty works in his disciples'

presence which are not written down in this book. [31] These have been written that you may believe that Jesus is the Messiah, the Son of God, and that through this faith you may have life in his name.

Jesus Appears to Seven Disciples

21 After this, Jesus showed himself once more to his disciples at Lake Tiberias. This is how he did it. [2] Simon Peter, Thomas (called the Twin), Nathanael (the one from Cana in Galilee), the sons of Zebedee, and two other disciples of Jesus were all together. [3] Simon Peter said to the others, "I am going fishing." "We will come with you," they told him. So they went and got into the boat; but all that night they did not catch a thing. [4] As the sun was rising, Jesus stood at the water's edge, but the

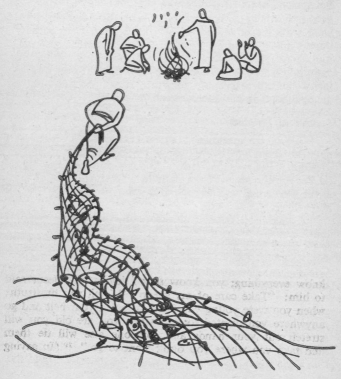

disciples did not know that it was Jesus. [5] Then he said to them, "Young men, haven't you caught anything?" "Not a thing," they answered. [6] He said to them, "Throw your net out on the right side of the boat, and you will find some." So they threw the net out, and could not pull it back in, because they had caught so many fish. [7] The disciple whom Jesus loved said to Peter, "It is the Lord!" When Simon Peter heard that it was the Lord, he wrapped his outer garment round him (for he had taken his clothes off) and jumped into the water. [8] The rest of the disciples came to shore in the boat, pulling the net full of fish. They were not very far from land, about a hundred yards away. [9] When they stepped ashore they saw a charcoal fire there with fish and bread on it. [10] Then Jesus said to them, "Bring some of the fish you have just caught." [11] Simon Peter went aboard and dragged the net ashore, full of big fish, a hundred and fifty-three in all; even though there were so many, still the net did not tear. [12] Jesus said to them, "Come and eat." None of the disciples dared ask him, "Who are you?" because they knew it was the Lord. [13] So Jesus went over, took the bread, and gave it to them; he did the same with the fish.

[14] This, then, was the third time Jesus showed himself to the disciples after he was raised from death.

Jesus and Peter

[15] After they had eaten, Jesus said to Simon Peter, "Simon, son of John, do you love me more than these?" "Yes, Lord," he answered, "you know that I love you." Jesus said to him, "Take care of my lambs." [16] A second time Jesus said to him, "Simon, son of John, do you love me?" "Yes, Lord," he answered, "you know that I love you." Jesus said to him, "Take care of my sheep." [17] A third time Jesus said, "Simon, son of John, do you love me?" Peter became sad because Jesus asked him the third time, "Do you love me?" and said to him, "Lord, you know everything; you know that I love you!" Jesus said to him: "Take care of my sheep. [18] I tell you the truth: when you were young you used to fasten your belt and go anywhere you wanted to; but when you are old you will stretch out your hands and someone else will tie them and take you where you don't want to go." [19] (In saying this Jesus was indicating the way in which Peter would die

and bring glory to God.) Then Jesus said to him, "Follow me!"

Jesus and the Other Disciple

20 Peter turned around and saw behind him that other disciple, whom Jesus loved — the one who had leaned close to Jesus at the meal and asked, "Lord, who is going to betray you?" 21 When Peter saw him, he said to Jesus, "Lord, what about this man?" 22 Jesus answered him, "If I want him to live on until I come, what is that to you? Follow me!" 23 So a report spread among the followers of Jesus that this disciple would not die. But Jesus did not say that he would not die; he said, "If I want him to live on until I come, what is that to you?"

24 He is the disciple who spoke of these things, the one who also wrote them down; and we know that what he said is true.

Conclusion

25 Now, there are many other things that Jesus did. If they were all written down one by one, I suppose that the whole world could not hold the books that would be written.

GOOD NEWS FOR MODERN MAN

The New Testament in Today's English Version

This translation in contemporary language, published originally in the United States by the American Bible Society, has met with wide approval. Over twenty-five million copies have been sold throughout the world.

Editions available in the United Kingdom Published by Collins and Fontana Books.

New Testament T.E.V.

Paperback illustrated	608 pp.		25p
Cloth	,,	,, ,,	60p
Rexine	,,	,, ,,	£1.38

Published jointly by the British and Foreign Bible Society and the National Bible Society of Scotland in association with Fontana Books.

New Testament without illustrations		15p
Single Books with illustrations		
Matthew	80 pages	3p
Mark	64 pages	3p
Luke	84 pages	3p
John	64 pages	3p
Philippians	16 pages	2p